HAT TRICKS

80 Instant Makeovers that Transform Ordinary Hats into Fabulous Creations

previous page:
The 'Bows and ties'
makeover for a picture hat
on page 13;

this page:
The sinamay band on
page 11 worn on its own;

contents page:
The 'Gold tissue silk'
cocktail hat on page 42

2

HAT TRICKS

80 Instant Makeovers that Transform Ordinary Hats into Fabulous Creations

TERENCE TERRY

Lark
Books

Contents

Dedication
To Maggie - a true believer -
with fondest memories

Design: Pentrix
Illustrations: Terence Terry
Photographer: Shona Wood

Published in the U.S.A. by Lark Books,
50 College St., Asheville, NC 28801
Distributed by Random House, Inc., in
the United States and Canada

Copyright © 1998 in text,
photographs, and illustrations
New Holland (Publishers) Ltd.
Copyright © 1998 in hat designs
Terence Terry.
All rights reserved.
Originally published in the U. K. by
New Holland (Publishers) Ltd.

Created and produced by
Rosemary Wilkinson Publishing,
London, England

Library of Congress Cataloging-in-
Publication Data
  Terry, Terence
    Hat Tricks: 80 instant makeovers
    that transform ordinary
    hats into fabulous creations
    /Terence Terry.
    p. cm.
    Includes index.
    ISBN 1-57990-038-0 (hc.) —
    ISBN 1-57990-039-9 (pbk.)
    1. Hats. 2. Millinery. I. Title.
TT657.T47   1998
646.5'04—dc21   97-39814
                              CIP
10 9 8 7 6 5 4 3 2 1

Introduction

*N*ot since the late fifties and early sixties has millinery been so popular. Fashionable stores are extending their departments to accommodate the ever-increasing demand for hats, including both high fashion items and street styles in a wide variety of shapes, colors and prices.

Hats are so prominent on the catwalks of Paris and Milan that a role reversal has taken place; instead of the millinery accessorizing the show outfits, couturiers are being requested to create clothes to complement hats by well-known designers. Choosing a hat can be quite difficult. It is best not to have a preconceived style in mind. Try on lots of different shapes and sizes to see what will suit you.

If you are choosing a hat for a particular outfit, take it along and check the balance and color against the hat. Also wear the correct shoes, as your heel height will affect the balance of the whole look and remember to check your back view: a large brim can dip so low that the neck can disappear and make you look a bit top heavy.

This book is designed to enable you to create simple and exciting changes to a favorite but possibly rather worn hat. A knowledge of simple sewing skills is useful as many of the makeovers are created without the use of a machine. I often find it easier to hand stitch and this doesn't flatten the fabric as a sewing machine tends to do. Basic techniques are, however, explained at the back of the book after a parade of over 80 everyday to exotic ideas which I hope will encourage you to personalize your own hat collection.

Brighten up a Straw Hat

by making a flower-studded band in a complementary color, adding ribbons and flamboyant feathers

Dull colors and lack of shape make this worn straw hat rather uninteresting.

This is a versatile hat for all ages. With different styling it can turn from being a fun hat to wear at the beach to an elegant hat for a summer wedding. Acrylic straw has the advantage that it is not damaged by rain and this hat with its unconstructed style can be worn with the brim up or down or half turned up and pinned. You can decorate it with all kinds of different embellishments: shells, flowers, hatpins, brooches and ribbons. The simplest decoration is just to turn the brim back on itself and stitch on a parchment flower. Choose a good bold flower and you instantly create a more dramatic hat.

The other great advantage of this hat is its understated coloring. It will tone in with many different outfits and can take extra decorations in a surprising range of strong and complementary colors.

For the main makeover, I have made a loosely folded band from sinamay. This is a stiff, loose-weave fabric, which can be molded into shape when wet and will hold the shape permanently once it has dried. It makes an ideal headband for this acrylic straw, giving form to the floppy crown and can even be worn on its own (see page 2).

You don't have to go looking in a specialist millinery department to find ideas for decorating the hat, there are colorful ribbons to be found in the stationery and gift departments. Alternatively, look in the furnishing fabrics department for upholstery braids.

Keep an open mind when you go shopping. If you see something you like, buy at least ³/₄ yard/³/₄ meter, as the average circumference of a crown is 22 in/56 cm.

making a fabric band

❶ Cut a strip of sinamay fabric on the bias, 10 x 36 in/25 x 90 cm. Submerge it in lukewarm water for a few seconds. (A cloudy size will come out.) Take out and drape round a pan, flowerpot or other large round container. Arrange the folds as desired, overlapping at the back to hide the joins. Leave to dry: it will take about 30 minutes.

❷ Remove the sinamay from the mold and place round the hat to fit. If it's not quite right, you can readjust the circumference by holding the band in the steam of a kettle for a few seconds, then make larger or smaller as required.

❸ Check the band on the hat again. When you are happy with the fit, stitch the back join of the sinamay to hold it in place.

❹ Take two sprays of tea roses (about 5 to a spray), cut to separate the roses and remove some of the leaves. Stitch to the folds of the sinamay band, concealing the end of one rose behind the rosebud of the next.

TRADE SECRETS

To restore body to a floppy straw hat, brush the inside with a fine layer of cellulose dope (varnish). It dries rapidly but remains flexible, so that you can still manipulate the brim.

build up a new style piece by piece by adding headbands, bows

1

1 Upfront purple.
A muted band and bow is given instant glamor just by adding a big spray of flowers. You will need one and a half yards or meters of printed ribbon.

Cut and fit a length for the headband the circumference of the crown plus seam allowances. Pull round the hat to fit, wrong side out, pin, then stitch the back seam off the hat.

For the bow, it helps to spray glue to the reverse of the ribbon to give it more body. Leave to dry, then form into a three-looped bow and bind the center with a small piece of ribbon with the sides folded in. Glue the bow to the front of the head-band, then simply stitch on the flowers.

2 South American style.
An alternative band for the hat can be quickly made from two braids. I have chosen a fringe and a braid in related colors.

You will need a length of each the circumference of the crown plus seam allowances. Stitch the braid on top of the fringe with a loose running stitch. Choose a neutral color and the stitches will not be obvious. Pull the band round the hat, pin the seam, then stitch off the hat. Trim the seam and lightly press to one side. Replace on the hat with the brim turned up slightly.

2	3
4	5

3 Sideways look.

Placing a flower at the side of the hat produces a quite different look: more elegant than dramatic.

Here the sinamay band has been molded into pleats and knotted, then placed with the knot at the side of the hat and a big flower stitched over the top.

4 Ruffled feathers.

Here is another very simple adaptation of the hat, which requires no stitching. These two hatpins are made from ostrich feathers. I've chosen soft colors to match the muted shades of the hat.

The great thing about these light feathers is the way they move as you turn your head. Where you place the hatpins can affect the style of the hat. I like to put them at the front, so that they are the center of attraction.

5 Ribbon and bow.

This style is designed for a teenager – it's simple and unfussy.

Make the headband and bow as described in 'Upfront purple'. Place the headband in position, then turn up the brim at the front and attach the bow. Stitch through all layers to hold the brim in position.

Dramatic Changes to a Picture Hat

by swathing it in bold contrasting colors and draping it with feathers

A plain picture hat in a good color but without any distinctive decoration.

This striking headband can simply be dropped over the crown of your hat, so you could make several different designs to match different outfits. First remove the existing trimmings carefully.

Measure the circumference of the crown and add $^{1}/_{2}$ in/1.5 cm plus seam allowances. Measure the depth of the crown and deduct $^{1}/_{2}$ in/1.5 cm, as you want the top of the crown to be just visible above the band. Cut a piece of buckram on the bias to these measurements. Overlap the two short ends by $^{1}/_{2}$ in/1.5 cm and stitch together with a large running stitch.

Cut a length of millinery wire and take out the bounce (see page 73). Attach to one of the edges of the buckram circle (now the top edge) with wire stitch. Cover this with a strip of bias-cut woven interfacing (see page 72). Cut a strip of batting 4 in/10 cm deep by the circumference of the crown. Fold in half lengthways and place to the inside of the circle, along the wired edge, aligning the folded edge to the top of the circle. Tack to hold. Cut another piece of batting the same length as before by the depth of the crown plus $2^{1}/_{2}$ in/6.5 cm. Place over the outside of the circle, butting the two short edges together to form the back join and aligning the bottom edge with the base of the circle. Whip stitch the back join. Tack along the bottom edge to hold in place. Fold over the excess at the top to cover the previous strip of batting. Tack again.

On the bias, cut a strip of band fabric, the depth of the crown plus 3 in/7.5 cm by the circumference plus seam allowances. Pull round the buckram circle, right side down and pin the back join. Remove, stitch the seam, then press to one side. Place over the circle, right side out, then fold the top and lower edges to the inside and glue in place.

variations on a theme

TOP
Bows and ties.

You will need 2 yards/2 meters of striped grosgrain and ³/₄ yard/³/₄ meter each of tartan and yellow satin ribbons. Use fusible web to bond the tartan and yellow ribbons together (see page 74). Make a headband from the striped ribbon, with the join at the front of the hat (see page 10). Tack the seam. Stitch the bonded ribbons into a circle. Fold with the seam in the center and gather through the seam. Make a slightly smaller bow from the grosgrain and stitch behind the first at an angle. Cut two 'tails' from the grosgrain, trimming the ends diagonally and stitch to the bows. Gather up the remaining striped ribbon into a rolled rose (see page 67). Stitch the rose over the bows, then stitch to the headband.

MIDDLE
Winged band.

This band of black textured PVC is basically made the same way as the padded band but is cut on the straight grain ¹/₂ in/1.5 cm taller and fitted without the batting. Make and wire the buckram circle as before. Pull the PVC round the buckram, pin and stitch as before. Turn under both edges and glue. Next cut a strip of buckram 1¹/₂ x 22 in /3.5 x 56 cm. Trim the short ends at a 45° angle. Wire all round with millinery wire and bind with a bias strip of interfacing (see pages 72 and 73). Cover with PVC and glue in place. For the knot, cut a 12 in/30 cm strip of buckram to the same depth. Cover with PVC as before. Tie into a loose knot and glue. Pin the knot and strip to the hat. Bend the ends into flowing wings. Remove from the hat, then cover the back with grosgrain ribbon in a contrasting color and also the inner top edge of the PVC band. Glue to the hat.

BOTTOM
Fine feathers.

Pin ³/₄ yard/³/₄ meter of ostrich feathers round the base of the crown leaving a small overlap, then trim off the excess. Attach a press stud to the ends of the band to join. Pop over the crown, then add the padded band.

13

Take One, Two or Three Berets

*and have fun embellishing them
with buttons and bundles of yarn
or join them together with
braid or decorative stitching
for a checkerboard effect*

*Plain berets provide
the perfect
foundation for a
riot of decorations.*

H ere is a new lease on life for all those mother-of pearl buttons saved from old blouses and shirts and squirrelled away. Stitch a select circle of buttons round the brim of the beret and the rest at random all over the surface. This type of decoration was made famous by the Pearly Kings and Queens of London. The number of pearl buttons stitched on their suits and hats was an indication of the extent of their wealth.

The buttons do not have to be stitched on individually, one length of the thread can be used to attach several but be sure to knot the thread securely after every third or fourth button, so that if the thread comes loose after several wearings, you will not lose all the buttons.

For a young child you could use novelty buttons in the shape of teddy bears or zoo animals. Pearl buttons catch the light and will match with any beret color but you could obviously try this adaptation with any kind of button.

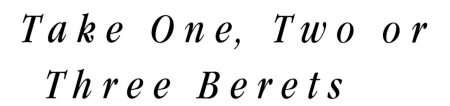

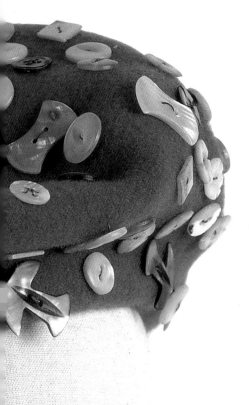

variations on a theme

TOP

Chenille bundles.

In this version the beret is embellished with loopings made from a ball of chenille yarn. Divide the brim of the beret with pins into twelve sections following the hours of a clock.

To make the loopings, wrap some chenille yarn twelve times round a bank card, then tie the loops together at the top with yarn to secure. Ease off the card. Repeat to make sixteen loopings in all. Stitch one of the loopings at the twelve o'clock position on the brim of the hat and another at six o'clock. Stitch the next two at three and nine o'clock, then gradually fill in the others at the remaining points of the clock. To finish, stitch a bundle of four loopings to the top center of the beret.

MIDDLE

Half and half.

This and the next hat feature variations made by amalgamating the two berets. Make a straight cut through the diameter of both berets. Butt one cream and one blue half together and whip stitch the join. Press, then cover the seam with a ³/₄ yard / ³/₄ meter strip of coordinating braid. Back stitch down both sides and take under to the inside. Trim the ends, leave raw but over stitch to neaten. Take ³/₄ yard / ³/₄ meter of matching fringed braid and roll up to make a pompom. Turn in the raw edge and stitch to secure. Place on top of the beret and stitch in place.

LOWER

A piece of pie.

A third beret in a darker blue was also used for this adaptation. Cut each of the remaining two halves into three equal segments. Cut a small circle from the top of the third beret including the 'stalk'. Cut six leaf shapes (see page 78) near the top from the remainder. The rest of the beret will be used for another hat.

Tack one leaf shape at an angle to each of the six sections. Machine stitch round all the edges with a medium zigzag stitch using variegated thread, then butt join the segments, alternating the colors, to make a complete beret shape. Machine stitch with a close zigzag to conceal the seams. Tack, then zigzag stitch the top circle in place. Finally, machine two rows of zigzag stitching round the headband.

A New Style for a Beach Hat

made by shortening the width of the brim and adding white lace, silk ribbons and organza ruffles

A plain, wide-brimmed straw, suitable as a fun hat but without a great deal of style.

The main change I made to this hat was to reduce the size of the brim to make it more sophisticated but first the straw needed to be freshened. To do this, I removed the trimmings, brushed the straw, then held it carefully over steam for a few seconds.

This type of hat is made from a continuous strip of woven straw, machine-stitched into shape. It is therefore simple to reduce the size of the brim just by unpicking the stitching, which usually starts at the back of the brim, and unravelling the straw until the required size is reached. I took off about 3 in/7.5 cm. Cut off the strip, then push the new end to the underneath of the brim and restitch to secure. Coat the whole surface with a layer of varnish to stiffen the hat.

From $^1/_2$ yard/$^1/_2$ meter of lace, cut a circle just larger than the diameter of the brim, then cut a circle out of the center just smaller than the diameter of the crown. Place over the hat to fit and cut into the inner edge if it is too tight against the crown. Smooth the lace over the brim and tack round the brim edge to hold. Cut a small piece of lace to decorate the crown. Trim carefully round the motifs. Place onto the crown and tack round the headfitting line. Graft the two pieces of lace together by slip stitching (see page 75). Attach the lace to the crown with a few holding stitches. Trim the lace level with the brim edge.

To bind the brim edge, measure the circumference of the brim and cut a bias strip of white satin to this measurement plus seam allowances and $3^1/_2$ in/9 cm wide. Place the strip round the brim edge to check for fit, then join the two short ends together on the straight grain. Fold in half lengthways, wrong sides together. Pin to the underside of the brim, with the raw edges aligned with the brim. Stitch into place $^1/_2$ in/1.5 cm from the brim edge, turn over to the top side and loosely slip stitch into place along the previous stitching line. Make a narrow rouleau (see page 74) from white satin to fit round the base of the crown. Attach to the hat, then fix a large silk rose to one side on the brim.

TRADE ▲ SECRETS

For a completely rigid form, after steaming, coat with a thin layer of clear or picture varnish and allow to dry. This will also give a glossy finish to the straw.

add style to the new brim shape with extravagant fringe

1

1 Knotted fringe.

This debonair adaptation is made from two remnants of cravat silk (which is woven 2½ in/ 6.5 cm wide).

For the headband, cut a bias strip of spotted silk, 7 in/17.5 cm wide to fit loosely round the crown. Pin the back seam, remove from hat, mark the seam, then open out and press flat.

From striped silk, cut a 2 x 9 in/5 x 23 cm strip, cut in half crossways, then trim both pieces to a sharp point. Place at both ends of the headband, the short straight edges aligned with the seam lines, and bond to the band with fusible web (see page 74). Cover the raw edges with satin stitch, then satin stitch another outline in a contrasting thread a machine foot distance away. Stitch the back seam, then place the band over the hat, turning under the raw edges at top and bottom.

To make the knot, cut a piece of striped silk, 25 x 8 in/63 x 23 cm. Pull away the threads to form a 3 in/7.5 cm deep fringe at both ends. Fold in half lengthways, wrong sides together. Stitch into a tube with a French seam (see page 74). Tie into a knot, then place on the headband over the seam and secure with a few stitches.

and multicolored organza ruffles

2 **Ruffled band.**
From 1 yard/1 meter of checked organza, cut a bias strip across the widest part and 10 in/25 cm deep, then cut a bias strip from the same amount of silk lining to the same width and 7 in/17.5 cm deep.

With right sides together, stitch the two short edges of the organza. Repeat with the lining. With right sides together, stitch the lining to the organza round one edge. Repeat on the other edge but leave a gap for turning through. Turn to the right side and slip stitch the gap closed.

Divide the band into four equal sections and do the same with the crown of the hat. Place the ruffle over the crown and match the four points. Secure with a few stitches at these points, then ruffle up the fabric in between and hold in place with a few more stitches.

Garnishing a Traditional Felt Pork Pie Hat

with bright and cheerful, home-made and glitzy, purchased decorations

This little hat in an unassuming brown is in good condition but needs brightening up.

I found this wonderful piece of tapestry velvet at a yard sale and thought it would be perfect to brighten up the self-effacing brown of this little pork pie hat. To make a strip for your own hat, measure the circumference of the crown and add $^3/_4$ in /2 cm seam allowances, then measure two thirds the depth of the crown plus the same seam allowances. Cut a strip of your chosen fabric to these measurements. As the sides of the crown of this hat are straight, the fabric can be cut on the straight grain. Place round the crown for fit, wrong side out, and pin along the center back seam line. Remove the band, stitch the back seam by hand or machine and press the seam open. This tapestry velvet would be too bulky if the seam were pressed to one side. Turn under the seam allowances at the top and bottom edges and her-ringbone stitch into place. Place over the crown and slip stitch in place if necessary.

Make a double-headed tassel from multi-colored double-knitting yarns as described opposite, to match the colors in the headband. Secure to the top of the crown with a large wooden button.

making a yarn tassel

❶ From a piece of stiff card, cut a rectangle 8 x 4 in/20 x 10 cm. Wrap a ball of rainbow-colored yarn 80 times round the card, then knot through the loops at the top with a spare piece of yarn. Remove from the card.

❷ Cut three lengths of blue yarn and braid to form a cord 9 in/23 cm long. Tie the braided cord round the loops, so that the knot hangs half way down the inside of the loops.

❸ Knot another piece of blue yarn 1 in/2.5 cm away from the top and bind round the loops closely for about $^1/_2$ in/1.5 cm. Knot and hide the ends under the binding.

❹ Leave 1 in/2.5 cm clear, then bind again with blue yarn for another $^1/_2$ in/1.5 cm and knot as before. The knot of the braided cord should be below the two bindings.

❺ Pull the braided cord at the top to draw up the tassel into a double head. Make a loose knot in the braided cord at the top of the tassel to secure. Cut the loops at the bottom and trim level.

use the whole surface of the hat as the background for a

1

1 Stars and jewels.
These spectacular motifs are available in craft nd sewing shops. Stitch them at random over the whole surface of the crown, interspersed with mirror crystal stars. They make a bright and exotic adaptation to the hat, particularly suitable for a teenager.

Any selection of glittering motifs could be used or you could decorate the hat with shiny beads or large sequins. You could even make pompoms from glitter yarns and stitch all over the hat.

iot of decorative visual effects

2

2 Bound yarn pipes.

Another fun variation suitable for a young hat wearer. Wrap ochre colored double knitting yarn 40 times round a small book measuring about 6 in/15 cm across.

Tie the loops together at the top with the same color yarn and remove from the book. Tie a piece of contrasting double knitting yarn 1½ in/4 cm from the top and bind closely round the loops for a short distance. Tie on another color and continue binding. Repeat the color changes, until the binding is about 1 in/2.5 cm from the base of the loops. Finish with a knot, tucked behind the binding to hide. Repeat to make a total of seven pipe shapes.

Take the remaining piece of spare beret from the variation on page 15, dampen it and iron to straighten. Alternatively, cut a piece of felt to fit round the base of the crown. Pull round the crown to fit, butting the back join. Remove and cut a wavy line along the top edge. Whip stitch the back join, then replace on the hat. Trim off the loops from the top and bottom of the pipes. Stitch one vertically over the back join of the headband, then stitch the others, evenly spaced round the crown.

Emphasize the Style of a Beach Straw Hat

by adding distinctive decorations with wooden beads and gold cord, rolls of raffia and even a circle of natural seaweed and poppy heads

This summer straw is in good condition but lacks any distinguishing features.

A selection of ethnic motifs made from beads and decorated with glitter adds the extra sparkle which this plain straw is lacking. Pin the motifs close together round the base of the crown, so that they are sitting just above the brim, then adjust the positions until they are evenly spaced.

Stitch down at the base and tip of each motif. Stitch large wooden beads in between each one in a circle round the hat.

Take three pieces of gold cord, 1 yard/1 meter long, knot them together about 3 in/7.5 cm from the ends, then braid. Leave about 3 in/7.5 cm unbraided and knot to secure the braiding. Place round the hat just below the base of the motifs and tie in a knot at the front. Trim off the ends of the cords neatly.

variations on a theme

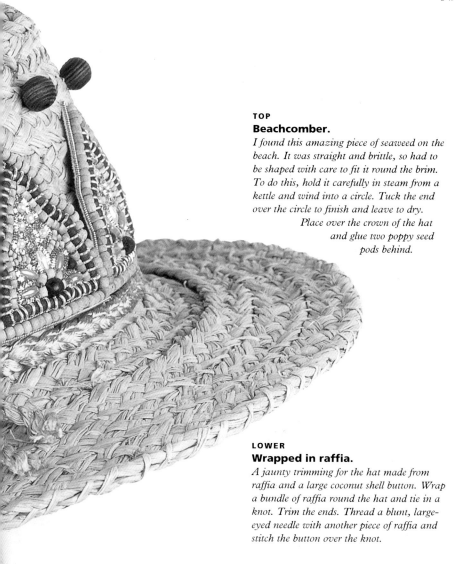

TOP
Beachcomber.
I found this amazing piece of seaweed on the beach. It was straight and brittle, so had to be shaped with care to fit it round the brim. To do this, hold it carefully in steam from a kettle and wind into a circle. Tuck the end over the circle to finish and leave to dry. Place over the crown of the hat and glue two poppy seed pods behind.

LOWER
Wrapped in raffia.
A jaunty trimming for the hat made from raffia and a large coconut shell button. Wrap a bundle of raffia round the hat and tie in a knot. Trim the ends. Thread a blunt, large-eyed needle with another piece of raffia and stitch the button over the knot.

TRADE SECRETS

A glue gun is very useful for securing small items to a hat. Use on this hat to attach seashells or other small finds from the seashore all over the surface .

25

Creating a New Cloche Hat

by reconstructing the brim, fitting fun fabrics over the crown and adding a touch of drama with feathers and angled bands

This cloche has a good shape but is otherwise very plain and understated.

If the hat is a little marked on the outside, it can simply be turned inside out. Remove the trimmings and the head ribbon, then cut away the brim from the crown $^3/_4$ in/2 cm below the headfitting line. Cut along the center back line of the cut-off brim to open it out, then press it flat with a hot iron. Take a pattern in woven interfacing from the flattened brim. The pattern is used to reshape the brim, which is cut so that there is a seam at the front. This seam is covered by the velvet lining, which is cut from the same pattern but so that the seam is at the back where it is not so visible. You will need $^1/_2$ yard/$^1/_2$ meter of velvet. Cut and line a new brim as described opposite.

Once you have cut and lined the new brim, tack round the outer brim edge to hold the lining and velvet together. Tack round the inner headline.

On the crown, trim along the lower edge using pinking shears, then snip vertically at the top of each 'V' shape to form a fringe $^1/_2$ in/1.5 cm deep.

Fit the brim inside the crown, so that the velvet is on the underside. Pin, tack, then machine stitch into place just above the fringe. Replace the head ribbon and remove all tacking stitches. Turn up the brim and hold in place on the crown with a few holding stitches. Spray the crown on the inside with a fine mist of fabric stiffener to give it body.

To make the feather trim, I used a new feather duster. Take out a handful of feathers, then bind them together with sticky tape and cover this with a piece of grosgrain ribbon, glued in place. Stitch the feathers to one side of the brim.

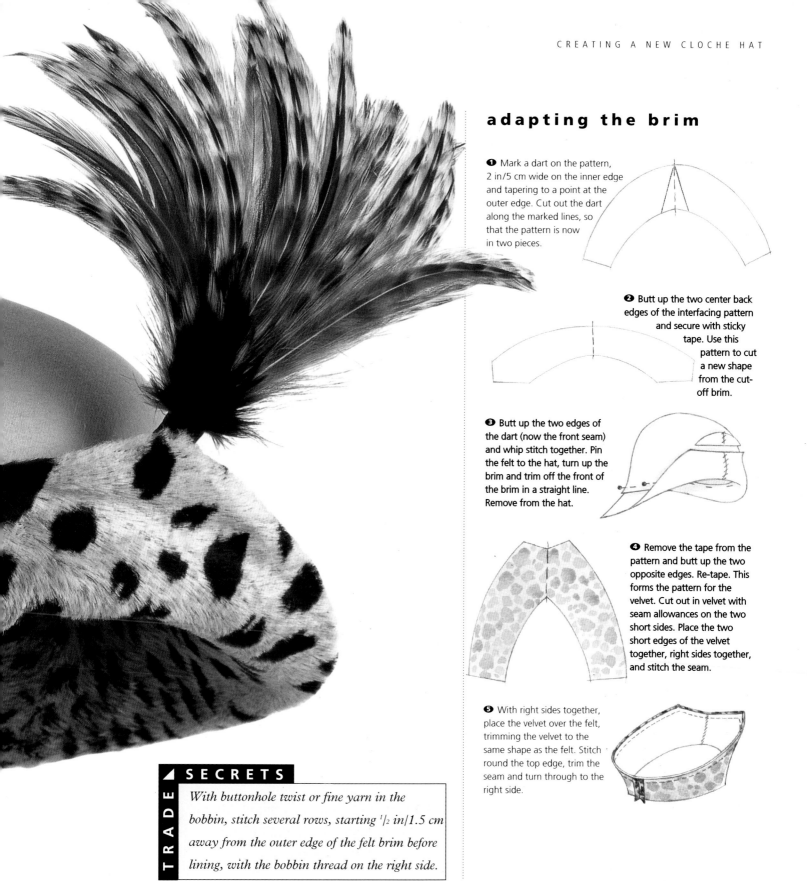

adapting the brim

❶ Mark a dart on the pattern, 2 in/5 cm wide on the inner edge and tapering to a point at the outer edge. Cut out the dart along the marked lines, so that the pattern is now in two pieces.

❷ Butt up the two center back edges of the interfacing pattern and secure with sticky tape. Use this pattern to cut a new shape from the cut-off brim.

❸ Butt up the two edges of the dart (now the front seam) and whip stitch together. Pin the felt to the hat, turn up the brim and trim off the front of the brim in a straight line. Remove from the hat.

❹ Remove the tape from the pattern and butt up the two opposite edges. Re-tape. This forms the pattern for the velvet. Cut out in velvet with seam allowances on the two short sides. Place the two short edges of the velvet together, right sides together, and stitch the seam.

❺ With right sides together, place the velvet over the felt, trimming the velvet to the same shape as the felt. Stitch round the top edge, trim the seam and turn through to the right side.

TRADE SECRETS

With buttonhole twist or fine yarn in the bobbin, stitch several rows, starting ¹/₂ in/1.5 cm away from the outer edge of the felt brim before lining, with the bobbin thread on the right side.

have fun with velvet to add a bold loop to the brim or

1

1 Loop with cord button.

Set aslant the turned-up brim, this loop adds a dash of style.

To make the loop, cut a piece of millinery buckram 20 x 2¼ in/51 x 5.5 cm, tapering to a point at one end. Bind the edges with a bias strip of woven interfacing (see page 72). Cover this with a piece of soft interfacing, folding the seam allowance to the underside. Glue to hold. Cut a strip of velvet on the bias and cover the interfacing as before. Line the shape with a piece of velvet, bonded to it with fusible web (see page 74). Fold 6 in/15 cm of the strip underneath and stitch in place.

To make the cream cord button, cut a circle 2 in/5 cm in diameter from millinery buckram. Form into a cone and bind the outer edge with a bias strip of woven interfacing (see page 73). Attach a length of cream cord just below the tip, then wrap the cord round the cone from top to bottom, stitching as you go. Glue the end of the cord to the inside to finish.

Place the button in position on the loop and stitch, then position the loop on the brim and stitch down with a couple of holding stitches.

make a smart satin headband

2

2 **Two-tone band.**
Measure the circumference of the crown, add seam allowances then cut a piece of black duchesse satin on the bias to this length and 3 1/2 in/9 cm deep.

Cut a piece of 1 in/ 2.5 cm wide grosgrain ribbon the same length and bond (see page 74) to a piece of brown satin which has seam allowances on all sides. (If the crown is shaped, curve the ribbon first, see page 72.)

Turn in the long edges of the brown satin and glue. Place onto the black satin about one third of the way up. Stitch the back seam.

Turn in the long edges of the black satin and tack to hold. Make a horizontal tuck at the back of the band. Cover the back seam with a little piece of brown satin, then place the band round the hat.

cover the crown and create new opportunities for bold

3

3 Covered crown.
Measure the circumference of the crown at the base of the headline and add seam allowances. Cut a piece of fabric on the bias to this measurement and about 11 in/ 28 cm deep. Tack and stitch the two short edges together on the straight grain to form a tube (see page 74). Fold the tube flat and, with right sides together, stitch across the top edge taking a $^3/_4$ in/ 2 cm seam allowance. Open out the tube and turn under $^3/_4$ in/2 cm at the lower edge. Machine or hand stitch in place, then turn through to right side.

Place over the crown and pin along headfitting line. Fold down one corner to the front of the crown and the other to the back. Pin, when satisfied with positioning. Remove from the hat and stitch down the corners. Replace and slip stitch in position. Turn up the brim and secure to the crown. Attach a tassel to the back corner.

changes to the original shape

4

4 Peaked hat.
Make the covering as above but stitch down only one of the corners. Maintain the point of the other with a piece of boning stitched to the inside.

You could also make this or the makeover opposite in black satin.

Alternatively, you could make a circular covering for the crown by cutting a 24 in/61 cm diameter circle from crushed velvet and gathering it up to fit the crown with a piece of elastic threaded through the hem. Place the circle over the crown and arrange tucks and folds in it, held in place with a few holding stitches.

Elegant Variations on a Plain Grey Toque

made by trimming the hat in satin and adding a trio of quills, by attaching an elegant overblown rose, lace-trimmed velvet, pheasant plumes or a new fake fur casing

Without any embell-ishments, this toque is a smart but rather insignificant hat.

Remove the head ribbon. Cut a length of pleated ribbon to fit round the base of the hat plus seam allowances, then machine stitch round the top edge of the ribbon, using a narrow zigzag stitch, to give a fluted finish to the ribbon. Place the straight (lower) edge of the ribbon round the crown 1 in/2.5 cm from the bottom and make a neat join at the back.

Cut a piece of grey satin on the bias, 3 in/7.5 cm wide by the circumference of the crown plus seam allowances. Stitch the back join of the satin band on the straight grain (see page 74). Trim and press open. Place the band over the crown of the hat, right sides together and aligning the lower edges. Using a long holding or tacking stitch, stitch the band to the hat being sure to catch the lower edge of the pleated ribbon. Turn down the band and fold back to the inside of the crown. Stitch down on the previous stitching line, then replace the head ribbon.

Peel off the barbs from three black feathers. Spray the quills with black paint to cover any white marks. Sandwich the quills between a pair of black cord frogs (normally used for dressmaking) and glue or stitch to hold in place. Attach the quills to the side of the hat.

variations on a theme

TOP

Cossack style.

If the side of your toque is an irregular shape, as here, you will need to take a pattern of the shape. Cut a piece of tracing paper or interfacing and place round the hat. Pin in place round the widest part, i.e. the top of the crown. Cut the pattern from the base to just below the top of the crown at regular intervals and overlap the sections until the pattern fits the crown. Draw a line round the top, bottom and center back seam. Remove from the hat, press flat and cut round the marked lines.

Use the pattern to cut a piece from fake fur, adding $1^{1}/_{2}$ in / 4 cm seam allowances all round. It's wise to cut fur slightly bigger than normal to allow for the thickness of the pile. With right sides together, tack the center back seam. On the right side, tease out the fur pile trapped within the seam, then check for fit on the hat. Machine or hand stitch the seam. Tease out any pile trapped in the seam, to form an invisible join. Turn the top and base seam allowances to the wrong side and herringbone stitch into place.

If the hems at top and bottom make the band uneven, the fur fabric can be mounted on a layer of batting, cut to the same pattern without seam allowances and loosely attached to the wrong side of the fur.

Place the fur band over the hat and slip stitch into place. For the feather trim, make a deep cone cut from a $3^{1}/_{2}$ in / 9 cm circle of millinery buckram and cover with grey velvet (see page 73). Bind together a bunch of feathers, then push into the cone. Provided they are a tight fit, they will not need to be stitched or glued in place. This also makes them easier to store when the hat is not in use. Attach the feathers to the hat using a Celtic pin.

LOWER

Feather fantasy.

Take two pheasant feathers. Bend the tip of each to the base and hold carefully in steam for a few seconds to set the shape. Catch in position with a few stitches. Place the two feathers together to form a figure-eight, place in position on the hat and stitch. Pin a brooch over the join, then tease out the barbs to give a distressed look to the feathers.

keep it formal with a smart velvet collar or a subdued

1

1 Contrast velvet collar and cone.

Using the pattern made for the Cossack style hat, draw the collar shape as shown in the photograph, with a slightly curved 'V'. Cut out the shape in millinery buckram without any seam allowances. Bind round all the edges with a bias strip of woven interfacing (see page 72), then cover with a bias strip of soft interfacing. This can be glued in position. Cut a piece of velvet to this shape but including seam allowances on all sides. Place over the buckram and fold over the raw edges, clipping to fit if necessary and taking great care at the base of the 'V'. Glue into place. Butt the back seam together and whip stitch by hand.

Stitch a strip of black lace on the outside of the crown along the base, so that it hangs below the crown. Place the velvet collar in position, hiding the lace edge and stitch round the base line.

From the pattern on page 77, make a velvet-covered cone (see page 73) and stitch in place at the top of the crown.

To finish, stitch a button at the base of the 'V' shape on the collar.

atin rose in muted colors

2

2 Fabric flower.

Cut a bias strip of grey satin brocade, 3 x 60 in/ 7 x 150 cm. Fold in half lengthways, wrong sides together. Pin, then tack in a diagonal line from $^{1}/_{2}$ in/1.5 cm above the folded edge at one end, rising to the top raw edges at the other. Make into a gathered rose, starting at the narrow end (see page 67). Place the rose on an ironing board, face up, cover with a cloth and press lightly with a steam iron to flatten.

Cut four leaf shapes (see page 78) from the satin and bond together in pairs using fusible web (see page 74). Machine stitch the central vein of the leaf using a narrow zigzag stitch, then, using the machine foot as a guide, zigzag round the outer edges. Trim away the fabric close to the stitching. Stitch a narrow pleat at the base of each leaf, then join the two leaves together and attach to the rose.

Cut a length of millinery wire 16 in/ 41 cm long and turn over the two ends. Make a rouleau from a strip of grey satin 1 $^{1}/_{2}$ x 16 in/ 4 x 41 cm long (see page 74). Place the wire inside the rouleau and neaten the ends. Bend the rouleau in half and attach to the back of the rose. Pin and stitch to the hat.

New Looks for an Italian Straw Breton

by making a simple, dramatic, orange silk bow and adding colorful artificial flowers

This Breton had lost its turned-up brim and needed some contrasting colors to bring it to life.

First remove all the trimmings. Turn the brim down by holding it briefly over steam, then ironing it flat. Next cut three bias strips, 7 x 32 in/18 x 80 cm, from orange organza. Place all three together lengthways, wrong sides together. Tack, then machine along the two long edges, taking a $^3/_8$ in/1 cm seam. Trim the seam back to $^1/_4$ in/0.5 cm. Turn through to the right side and tack along both seam lines to hold in place while you're making the bow. Overlap the two short sides and stitch. Cut another bias piece of organza 8 x 8 in/20 x 20 cm and fold two sides to the back to meet in the center. Loop round the bow with the raw edges at the back and stitch to hold.

Cut a headband in organza on the bias, 12 in/30 cm wide by the circumference of the crown plus seam allowances. Fold over about $^3/_4$ in/2 cm on both long edges, one to the front and one to the back. Fold in half, wrong sides together, then fit round the crown of the hat and stitch the join. Stitch the bow over the join. Slot in the sweet peas. The bow is set at an angle on the hat and can be loosely stitched in place at the top of the crown and to the brim.

variations on a theme

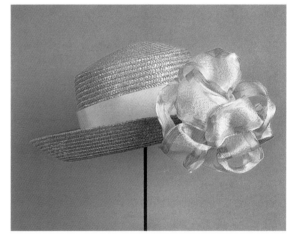

TOP
Exotic grasses.
Loosely stitch the brim onto the crown at the front and stitch on exotic grasses, with the stems fitted into wooden beads.

MIDDLE
Gift-wrapped.
Cut a headband from 1   in/4.5 cm wide grosgrain ribbon and fit round the crown. Make a decorative parcel bow with wire-edged ribbon and stitch to the brim edge.

LOWER
Autumn colors.
Bind a strip of autumn berries round the hat, bend the two wires together at the back and pop over the brim.

Bring New Life to a Floppy Purple Hat

with a variety of fun trimmings from little padded cushions to jazzy pins and brooches

This everyday hat is rather ordinary without any added decorations.

Bond together two ¹/₄ yard/¹/₄ meter pieces of silk in contrasting colors, using fusible web (see page 74) and keeping the grain of both in the same direction. I used maroon and grey. Cut out 18 petals on the bias using the template on page 77.

Cut two pieces of wire 9 in/23 cm long and fold over both ends. Cover one end with a piece of interfacing to pad. Cut two circles 2³/₄ in/7 cm in diameter from the bonded silk. Fold one of the circles in four so that the grey side is uppermost and place over the top of the wire to form the rosebud. Stitch it in place.

Fold one of the petals round the bud, grey side out, and stitch at the base. Repeat with seven more petals, placing them round all sides of the bud. Repeat to make a second rose but using the reverse side of the bonded silk.

Bind the length of both wires with a bias strip of grey silk. On one of the stems add the leaf shape, cut using the template on page 76 and stitch in place.

Put both roses together and stitch in place at the side of the hat.

TOP
Padded cushions.

First make a series of square and circular shiny cushions. To do this you will need five remnants of metallic cotton. Cut two squares 3 in/7.5 cm wide from three of the fabrics and two circles 3 in/7.5 cm in diameter from the remaining two. Cut three squares and two circles from lightweight batting to the same size. Place two squares of the same fabric, right sides together and a square of batting on top. Stitch round all sides, leaving an opening to turn through. Trim the batting close to the stitching and turn through, so that the batting is enclosed between two pieces of top fabric. Slip stitch the opening closed. Repeat with the two remaining squares and the two circles. Top stitch different patterns on each cushion to decorate. I made a spiral, a checked grid, a shell and a cross. Arrange the cushions in a group with the three squares in the middle and a circle at each end. Pin, then stitch into one unit at the back. Place over the crown and brim of the hat and stitch in a few places to secure.

MIDDLE
Papier mâché pins.

On the upturned brim and crown, pin a selection of brightly decorated papier mâché brooches and pins.

LOWER
Shirred band.

From elastic shirred fabric, make up a deep headband to fit round the side band of the crown (see page 10). Stitch the back join. Turn under the raw edges and herringbone stitch in place. Slip over the crown.

variations on a theme

Changing the Shape of a White Summer Straw Hat

by cutting away the brim and adding a profusion of flowers, or swathing the crown in red velvet, pleated silk and chiffon

A very ordinary summer hat, suitable for everyday wear but without glamor.

I have radically changed the shape of this hat by cutting off the brim and using the resulting pillbox shape as the foundation for transformations that turn it from an everyday hat into a series of glamorous creations for special occasions.

Remove the trimmings and head ribbon. Cut away the brim from the crown at the headfitting line, then turn under about ³/₄ in/2 cm and put in an easing thread (see page 72). Cut through the center back of the discarded brim and use this piece to make a strap for the hat, as described opposite. The strap is used for two of the makeovers; for the others the hat is held on with a little comb stitched inside the crown.

Once you have fitted the strap to the crown, take two long sprays of silk flowers and arrange them round the base of the crown and over the strap at one side of the hat. Stitch in place, hiding the stitches under the next flowers as you go. Fill out any spaces with more leaves glued in position.

To finish, replace the head ribbon inside the crown.

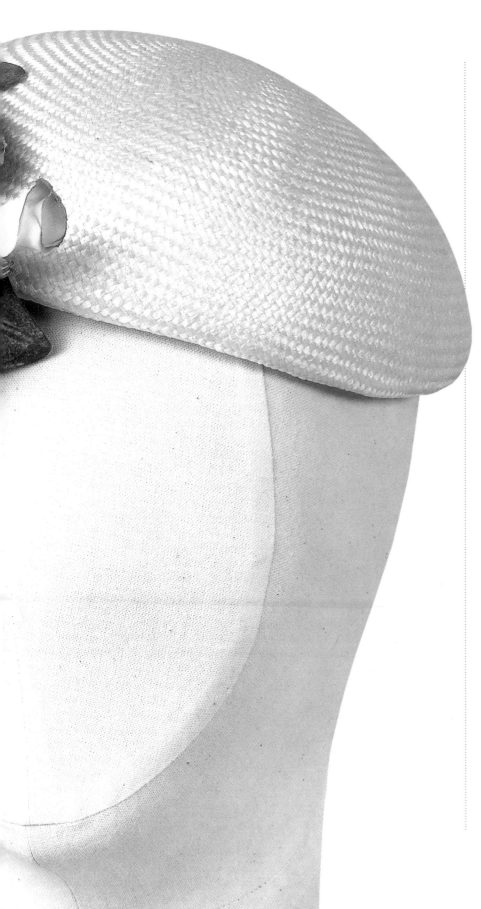

making a strap

❶ Cut through the center back of the cut-off brim, then, using a steam iron, gradually flatten out the circle until you have a rectangle.

❷ From this rectangle, cut a strip 3 in/7 cm wide across the length of the rectangle.

❸ Fold both the long raw edges into the center, then bring the two folded edges together and press. Slip stitch or glue the folded edges together.

❹ Pin the two short ends together to make a circle. Place the crown of the hat on top at an angle and, when satisfied with the position, pin the circle to the crown and cut off the excess circle inside the brim. Stitch in place.

use the original   crown as the base for fantastic

1

1 Gold tissue silk.
I've used hand-dyed, pleated metallic tissue silk for this spectacular cocktail hat (without the strap). You will need a piece of fabric the length of the circumference of the crown plus seam allowances and 30 in/ 76 cm deep. With right sides together, stitch the 30 in/76 cm sides together to make a circle. Turn to the right side, then fold in half, with raw edges together and wrong side inside. Place over the crown of the hat, arrange the pleats to fit round the headfitting line, then pin to the inside. Stitch in place. Bunch up the fabric at the top of the crown and hold in place temporarily with string.

To make the 'tails', cut two shapes (see pages 76-77) from millinery buckram. Wire the long straight edge, then bind all edges with a bias strip of interfacing (see pages 72 and 73). Bond a piece of bias-cut interfacing to one side of each tail (see page 74). Bond each tail to the wrong side of a strip of velvet large enough to allow for turnings on all sides. Turn over all edges and glue in place. Make a little band to fit round the center of the bunched fabric in the same way. Stitch the two tails together at the base and insert in the center of the organza tube.

Using double thread, bind the base of the

new fabric coverings in silk and chiffon

2

bunched fabric also securing the tails. Wrap the velvet band round and stitch the back join neatly. Group a selection of wired glass leaves and flowers into an irregular bunch by twisting the stems together. Stitch onto the velvet band at the front. Add the head ribbon and a comb to finish (see page 74).

2 Swathed in chiffon.
Just one chiffon scarf can be used to cover the hat and make the roses.

Place the crown of the hat in one corner of the chiffon scarf and pin. Pull the scarf smoothly over the crown to the opposite side and pin. Repeat at the two side points of the crown. Continue to ease out the fullness of the scarf and pin to the hat until it lies completely flat over the crown. Tack to the inside along the head-fitting line and trim off the excess scarf.

Cut a strip on the bias to fit over the straw strap. Glue to the strap. From the remaining fabric, cut out three bias strips 6 in/ 15 cm wide and as long as you can. Fold in half, then make into rolled roses (see page 67). The size of the rose will depend on the length of the strip. Stitch into position at the front of the hat, then attach a spray of matching feathers.

make the most of special fabrics to add panache to the

3

3 Pleated satin cover-up.

From one end of a half yard/half meter of pleated navy taffeta, cut a circle large enough to cover the top of the crown and tack in place. Trim the edges of the remaining piece so that you have a rectangle.

Fold in half with wrong sides together. Place the center back to the center back of the hat with the folded edge at the top, so that about 2 in/5 cm of the fabric hangs down below the brim.

Bring the sides round to the front of the hat, pinning to the side of the crown as you do so. Bring the top of one short edge down to the bottom edge, so that you have a fold on the bias. Repeat with the opposite side, then overlap both sides in a 'V' shape at the front and pin.

Stitch the raw edges to the inside of the crown and trim off all the excess fabric.

Fill the inside of this fabric wrap with about a dozen purple rose heads, glued or stitched in place on the tip of the crown. Take a yard/meter of millinery veiling, knot at the back, then arrange over the hat and catch stitch down.

Add the head ribbon and finish with a comb to hold (see page 74).

simple shape of the crown

4 Plush red velvet.
Using the templates on page 77, make seven small cones and one medium-sized from millinery buckram (see page 73). Cover with a layer of interfacing (without seam allowances) and glue in place. For each cone, cut a circle of red velvet large enough to cover the cone and fold to the inside. Place centrally over the cone and pull smoothly over the surface. Fold the raw edge to the inside and glue. Cut a circle of sparkled georgette and use to cover each cone in the same way.

Cut a large circle of red velvet about 15 in/ 40 cm in diameter and place centrally over the crown of the hat (without the strap).

Stitch the medium-sized cone in the center of the crown, stitching round the edges. Ruche up the velvet round the cone. Place the remaining seven cones evenly around, ruching up the fabric into folds in between. Stitch the cones in place. Secure the velvet folds with a few holding stitches. Turn the velvet to the inside of the crown and stitch down. Add several glass teardrops round the front of the crown. Add the head ribbon and finish with a comb to hold (see page 74).

Dressing up a Fur-trimmed Felt Hat

with a new range of coverings for the brim in soft blue fur, printed jersey, gold satin and purple silk

A well-worn winter hat which needs freshening up with contrasting colors.

Remove the head ribbon, then carefully unpick and remove the fur fabric from the brim. Lay flat and press. You can now either use this piece as a pattern, or take a paper pattern from it. Note the seam allowances and stitching lines.

Use the pattern and cut out a new trimming on the bias from gold satin. Stitch the back join, then place over the brim and tack down just below the top of the brim. Pull out the fullness towards the headfitting line and tack, then stitch round the inside edge. Place a bead-studded braid at the top edge of the brim, allowing the looped edge of the braid to stand just above the edge. Stitch in place on the edge of the brim along the original stitching line, then slip stitch the lower edge. At the back, fold over the short raw edge and stitch neatly down. To make a cockade of ostrich feathers, you'll need a ³/₄ yard/³/₄ meter length of ostrich feather. Simply roll this up and stitch at the base to hold. Stitch or pin to the crown of the hat behind the brim. Replace the head ribbon.

variations on a theme

TOP
Printed jersey.

Place the brim pattern on the bias on a piece of printed jersey and cut out. Stitch the two short sides together to form the back join. Place right side down behind the brim, aligning the raw edge with the top of the brim and stitch into place. Fold over the upper brim to the inside and attach to the headfitting line. Stitch or glue into place and replace the head ribbon. For the headband, cut a bias strip of jersey to fit the crown plus seam allowances and 12 in/30 cm wide. With right sides together, stitch the back join. Turn under 1 in/2.5 cm on the top and lower edges and tack to hold. Place over the crown and arrange tucks and folds in the head-band. When satisfied with the arrangement, hold in place with a few stitches and remove all tacking stitches.

MIDDLE
Cool blue.

If you are replacing one fur with another, as here, make sure that the new fur is of the same thickness as the original, otherwise you will alter the size of the headfitting line. Place your pattern on the chosen fur on the bias. Pin and cut out. Whip stitch the back join, then place the fur to the inner side of the brim, right side up. Pin, tack and stitch to the brim. Roll the fur over to the upper side of the brim. Pin the free edge along the original stitching line, trim, then glue into place. Replace the head ribbon. Attach a pendant brooch to the side of the brim.

LOWER
Threaded with purple silk.

Make six horizontal cuts in the edge of the brim evenly spaced and 1 in/2.5 cm below the brim edge. From 1 yard/1 meter of purple silk, cut a bias strip across the widest part, 10 in/25 cm deep. With right sides together, stitch along the long edge to make a tube. Trim, then turn through to the right side. Starting and finishing at the back, feed this tube through the incisions, wrapping the silk over the brim edge. Hide the joins underneath each other and put in a couple of stitches to hold. Replace the head ribbon.

Revive a Pretty Coral Felt Hat

by making decorations round the crown cut from other discarded felt hats and elegant snake skins the new focus

This simple felt hat has lost its freshness through constant wearing.

This principal makeover cleverly combines two felt hats: one a pink felt in good condition, the other a worn black one of similar size. Remove all trimmings, then cut off the crown from the black hat $2^1/_2$ in/6 cm from the head fitting line and cut away the brim at approximately the same distance from the headline. Snip into the cut crown and brim to form a fringe, then pop this band over the pink hat.

From the remainder of the black brim, cut out two large, curved feather shapes. Place together at the base and stitch to secure. Cut out narrow 'V' shapes along both edges of both feathers to resemble the barbs.

Cut another small piece of felt to wrap round and cover the end of the feathers. Cut one edge of this piece (the top edge) in a zigzag, then wrap round the end of the feathers and stitch in place.

Place the feathers into the front of the headband and catch down to the crown with a couple of holding stitches.

Fluff out the fringes of the black headband.

variations on a theme

TOP
Toning felt lilies.

Felt hats are easy to find in secondhand shops, so I have made use of another hat in a deeper pink to cut out a lily and leaves to decorate the original hat. Cut off the tip of the crown from the deeper pink hat, then cut out the calla lily shape using the template on page 76. From the side band section, cut three leaves, large, medium and small (see page 76). Straighten out the old brim with a steam iron, then fit round the hat to make a new headband and stitch. Place round the hat with the join at the front.

Using a medium zigzag stitch, machine down the center of each leaf in a contrasting thread. Take a 3 in/7.5 cm long piece of 1 in/2.5 cm wide yellow grosgrain ribbon and fringe one end. Roll this up lengthways, then lay in the center of the lily shape, aligning the unfringed end with the base. Stitch in place. Roll in the edges of the lily shape at the base and stitch, then fold over the top edge. Put a loose tuck half way down each leaf and stitch to hold. Pin the lily to the front of the headband. Cover the base with the largest leaf, place the medium leaf to the right and the smallest to the left. Stitch in place.

LOWER
Water snake skin.

This simple transformation just uses two snake skins, one red and one brown. Place the red snake skin round the base of the crown, overlapping the short ends and turning under the raw edges. Stitch in place. Fold the brown snake skin in half, then stitch in place on top of the red one, turning under the short edges at the back as before. Pin a papier mâché African mask to the crown to finish, if desired.

New, Improved Trimmings for a Peachbloom Felt Hat

with softly rolled roses, decorated ribbon headbands, bold rosettes and an abundance of flowers

A felt hat with a good shape but low-key trimmings.

Remove the trimmings carefully. This main transformation has a new padded headband, a bow and three softly gathered roses all in the same striped silk fabric. Steam and brush the hat to revive and freshen the felt (see page 72).

For the headband, cut a bias strip of fabric from $^3/_4$ yard/$^3/_4$ meter of silk, 4 in/10 cm wide and the circumference of the crown plus seam allowances. With right sides together, stitch along the long edge to make a tube, then turn through to the right side. Do not press. Cut a piece of batting 4 in/10 cm wide and the same length as the fabric tube. Feed through the tube. Place the padded band round the hat, pin the back seam, remove from the hat and stitch the seam. Trim the excess fabric, neaten the seam and press the seam to one side.

To make the bow, cut a bias strip 4$^1/_2$ x 30 in/12 x 76 cm. With right sides together, stitch along the long edge to make a tube, then turn through to the right side, making sure that the seam runs in the middle of one of the sides. This will be the reverse side. Stitch the two short ends together to form a circle. Flatten the circle, so that the seam is in the center and stitch down at this point, making two loops. To make the double bow effect, push in the ends of each loop to make a tuck and secure with a few stitches. Attach the bow to the headband at the center front.

To make the roses, cut three bias strips across the widest part of the fabric, 5 in/13 cm wide. Fold one of the strips in half lengthways and pin together. Gather across the top just below the raw edges but start the gathering stitches at the base of the strip near the fold and work up to the top edges in a smooth curve. Trim near to the stitching. Gathering up the stitches as you go, begin rolling into a rose shape and stitch to hold in position at the base. Finish as you began by curving the gathering stitches down to the folded edge. Repeat to make two more roses. Stitch the roses on top of the bow, concealing any raw edges.

▲ SECRETS

T R A D E

To store peachbloom felt hats, pad with layers of tissue paper and store upright in a hatbox. This prevents the delicate bloom from being damaged or marked.

use silver and   glitzy fabrics as the focus of attention

1

1 The maharajah.
The central rosette is
made from three short
lengths of fabric cut on
the straight of grain
which gives a more
angular effect.

Cut three strips,
3 x 20 in/7.5 x 50 cm.
Fold each strip in half
lengthways. Gather and
roll up the strips as
described on page 67.
When completed, stitch
the three mini rosettes
together.

For the fan you will
need two pieces of fabric
7 x 16 in/18 x 40 cm.
Bond the two fabrics
together with fusible web
(see page 74). Make a
pattern from shape 1 on
page 77 and cut out from
this fabric. Bind the two
straight edges with wired,
sticky-backed ribbon (see
page 73). Gather the
curved edge using a
double thread and pull
up into a fan shape. From
the remaining bonded
fabric, cut a narrow point
using pattern 2 from page
77. Bind both straight
edges as before, mitering
the pointed end.

Place the fan shape and
'tail' behind the rosettes
and secure with a few
holding stitches. Place on
the hat at a central point
and glue or stitch down.
Adjust the wired edges of
the fan and tail until you
have a pleasing shape.

set against the plain black background

2

2 All that glitters.
You will need a remnant of glitzy fabric 4 in/10 cm deep by the circumference of the crown plus generous seam allowances.

Pull round the crown of the hat and pin the back seam but not too tightly. Remove and mark the seam on both sides, then take out the pins. Fray the lower edge of the fabric to give a fringe about 1 in/2.5 cm deep. Try not to break the pulled-out threads and keep to one side. Machine stitch with a shallow zigzag just above the fringe to secure the remaining threads, then stitch the back seam and press open.

On the top edge, fold over $^3/_4$ in/2 cm and tack. Place the band over the hat and remove the tacking threads.

Fold the bundle of reserved threads in half and half again, they should measure about 8 in/20 cm deep. Tie together at the center and cut through the loops at both ends. From the original remnant, cut another piece $1^1/_4$ x 2 in/3 x 5 cm, fold in three lengthways and stitch down the raw edge. Wrap round the tassel, overlapping at the back, then trim off the excess fabric and stitch in place. Turn the tassel so that one layer flops over the other and attach to the hat with a hat pin.

make and decorate a new headband or add a bright posy

3

3 Embroidered ribbon.

A striking headband made from two grosgrain ribbons, one black and one cream with a third peach ribbon used for the appliquéed leaf shapes. The ribbons are 1½ in/ 4 cm wide. Place the black ribbon over the cream one overlapping by ¼ in/0.5 cm and machine stitch together.

As the crown of the hat is tapered, the ribbon will need to be shaped (see page 72). Place the ribbon round the crown to check for fit and repeat as necessary.

Cut out the leaf shapes (see page 78) from peach ribbon and bond to the two-tone headband using fusible web (see page 74). Using a contrast colored thread, stitch the central vein of the leaves using a narrow zigzag, then stitch round the edges of the leaves using a wider zigzag to conceal the raw edges.

Place the band round the hat, wrong side up, and pin the back seam. Remove and stitch the seam, then cover the seam with a narrow folded strip of peach ribbon, turning under the raw edges and securing on the reverse of the band. Replace on the hat.

# of flowers to embellish an elegant hat

4

▢ Pansies and buttercups.

A simple decoration for the hat: the secret is to choose really vibrant flowers to make a bold statement.

You will need two sprays of velvet pansies and one of buttercups. Place the buttercups in the middle and the pansies on either side with the stems facing inwards. Twist the wires together and bind with cotton thread to hold. Place the flowers diagonally across the front of the hat and stitch in place.

If you're going to a really special occasion, ask a florist to make up a spray of fresh flowers to pin to the hat.

A Glamorous Makeover for a Paper Straw Hat

made by adding voluptuous bows, a new headband and a profusion of flowers

A plain, unadorned, everyday summer hat: a perfect base for a new image.

From 1 yard/1 meter of white cotton organdie, cut two bias strips, 3 1/2 in/ 9 cm wide and as long as possible. Moisten the thumb and forefinger on both hands, then, starting at one end of one of the long edges, gently roll over the organdie to the right side until it forms a tight roll. Repeat on the other long edges of both strips.

Decide how long you wish the loops of each bow to be. Note that one is slightly shorter than the other. Cut one of the organdie strips to these lengths. Join the two short edges of each strip to form a circle, fold in half with the seam in the middle, then place the shorter loop centrally on top of the longer. Gather through the center.

Make a headband from the second strip (see page 10). Iron out the rolled edges from the remainder, cut in half, then taper the ends to a point and re-roll the edges. Attach these tails to the bow and spray lightly with fabric stiffener. Stitch to the headband over the join and cover the center of the bow with a loop of organdie. Remove any old trimmings, then attach the new headband and bow to the hat. Finally, stitch a large yellow flower and a spray of red poppies to the hat over the bow.

variations on a theme

TOP

Silk splendor.

For the large bow, cut a bias strip of lavender silk 14 in/36 cm wide across a half yard/half meter of fabric. Join the two short edges across the straight grain (see page 74). Turn in the raw edges by approximately 2 in/5 cm. Fold so that the seam is in the middle. For the smaller bow, cut a bias strip of pink silk 9 x 30 in/23 x 76 cm and make into a bow in the same way.

   Gather through the center of each to form a butterfly bow, then stitch the two loops together, one on top of the other.

   To make a binding knot, cut a piece of pink silk, 1 x 2^1/$_2$ in/2.5 x 6 cm.

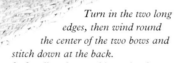

Turn in the two long edges, then wind round the center of the two bows and stitch down at the back.

   For the headband, cut a bias strip of lavender silk 6 x 27 in/15 x 68 cm. Fold in the two long edges and place round the crown. Pleat the two short edges and stitch together with a few holding stitches. Place the double bow over the join and stitch through to the hat to secure. To finish, wind 1^1/$_2$ yards/1^1/$_2$ meters of rosebud ribbon in a spiral from the tip of the crown to the brim, glueing down each end and at intervals along the length.

LOWER

Swathed in luminous fabric.

Metallic organza is impossible to iron once it is creased, so I have made a feature of this by deliberately scrunching up the fabric.

   Cut a circle of creased metallic organza 40 in/100 cm in diameter. Fold the circle in half, then place like a head scarf round the crown, making loose folds and tying it in a knot at one side. Trim and hide the raw edges beneath the knot. Turn under the raw edges at the base of the band, then insert the stem of a spray of white flowers into the knot and curve over the brim. Stitch in place with a few holding stitches.

Add a Touch of Luxury to a Brown Winter Felt Hat

with deep fur wraps, jaunty chopsticks, a ruched silk band, animal prints, a cockade of feathers and swirling taffeta

An old plain brown felt hat is a perfect foundation for exotic trimmings.

Measure the depth of the crown and add seam allowances. Measure the circumference of the crown and add really generous seam allowances, as the fabric being used is thick and the turned-over seams add considerable bulk. From 8 in/20 cm of deep pile fake fur, cut a piece on the straight grain to these measurements. Turn under the seam allowance on the two long edges and tack in place.

Place the band round the hat, right side out, to fit. Pin the back seam, then cut without seam allowances. Take the band off the hat, then remove tacking and open out. Butt the two short edges together and whip stitch the back join. Turn under the two long edges again and herringbone stitch on the wrong side to secure. Place the band over the hat (it does not need to be stitched in place).

Make a little bow from a remnant of striped satin ribbon and stitch to the front of the hat over the fur band. Alternatively, pin on a favorite brooch.

variations on a theme

TOP
Animal prints.

Animal print velvets are expensive but for this adaptation you only need a 4 in/10 cm strip or a remnant. Cut out leaf or feather shapes freehand from the velvet and pin to a piece of backing fabric, such as black satin. Satin stitch by machine round all the edges of the velvet shapes, then cut out the shapes close to the stitching.

Pin the shapes at random over the crown and the underside of the brim of the hat, then hand stitch invisibly into place. Turn up the brim and catch stitch to the crown.

MIDDLE
Chopsticks.

This corded figure-eight was a hairslide. I've replaced the original fixing with a pair of chopsticks. Turn up the brim of the hat and pin on the decoration at an angle with the chopsticks already in place, as this will make a difference to the shape. Stitch the bottom section of the hairslide to the brim and the top to the crown.

LOWER
A flight of fancy.

A simple but striking new look. Turn up the brim, place a spray of long brown feathers behind the brim and hold in place with a decorative brooch.

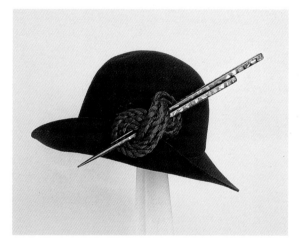

TRADE ▲ SECRETS

If the brim has become rather floppy from constant wearing, wire the edge and cover with a folded strip of grosgrain ribbon as described on page 73.

ruche silk or gather up taffeta to make captivating new

1 **Ruched silk.**
Roll a piece of light-weight batting 6 in/15 cm deep into a sausage shape and fit round the crown of the hat. Mark the back seam without any seam allowances, then trim off the excess fabric and whip stitch the long raw edge to secure.

Cut two bias strips of cravat silk 7 1/2 in/19 cm deep and to make a total length of 60 in/152 cm. Join the strips on the straight grain (see page 74) to form one long strip, then, with right sides together, stitch along the long edge to make a tube, trim and turn through to the right side.

Feed the batting sausage through the fabric tube, ruching up the fabric as you go but leaving 1 in/2.5 cm of batting free at each end. Butt the ends of the batting together and whip stitch, then pull over the silk to cover the join. Overlap the ends of the silk, turn under the raw edges of the top piece and slip stitch down. Adjust the ruching so that it is even over the length of the tube. Place over the hat, turn up the brim and catch stitch to the silk. Add a feather cockade if desired.

headbands the focus of attention

2

2 Soft satin bow.
From a $^1/_2$ yard/$^1/_2$ meter of olive shot taffeta, cut a strip 8 x 26 in/20 x 66 cm. Turn in the two long edges and press flat. Gather up the two short edges. Place round the hat, pin and stitch into place. Trim off the excess fabric.

Cut a second piece 8 x 16 in/20 x 40 cm and join the two short sides to make a circle. Fold under 1 in/2.5 cm on each long edge and press. Fold the circle in half with the seam in the middle, then gather through the seam and pull up. Gather again about 1 in/2.5 cm from each end of the bow and pull up loosely.

Add the bow to the headband, covering the join. Place over the hat and finish off with a metal button.

Finally, stitch metal buttons all over the crown.

Remodel a Neat Red and White Bowler Hat

to make it into a wedding hat, a fun hat or a young hat with gold tassels, white veiling and bright braids

A pretty shape and summery colors but lacking any eyecatching features.

I've used a purchased motif and two tassels for this makeover to show how you can make a feature of the trimming to add interest to a simple hat. I like decorations that move with the wearer and so draw attention to the hat. The colors chosen tone in with the colors of the hat rather than providing a stark contrast.

Stitch the two tassels to the reverse of the motif at opposite sides, so that the head of each tassel lies against the side of the motif. Place the motif and tassels in the center of the crown and stitch in place.

Instead of this type of motif, you could use nautical badges or other appliqué shapes, such as Celtic knots. Some of these are iron-on or adhesive-backed, which makes the transformation even easier.

You could use contrasting colors if desired and even spray the brim with an aerosol paint to match.

variations on a theme

TOP

Wedding veils.

Add a veil and instantly transform your hat into something perfect to wear for a wedding. Cut a piece of white veiling 36 in/1 meter long. (This is 11¹/₂ in/30 cm wide when sold.) Run a double gathering thread from the right hand bottom corner of one short edge diagonally up to the top edge, along the long edge and down to the bottom left hand corner (in the same way as for a rolled rose, see page 67). Trim off the excess veiling and pull up loosely. Stitch a large silk rose to the brim. Place the veiling over the rose and tuck the gathered edge under the brim, so that the two short gathered-up edges meet at the back. Catch stitch in place at various points round the brim.

MIDDLE

Upturned brim.

Simply by changing the shape of the brim, you can give this bowler a quite different style. Unroll the brim and bind the edge with red grosgrain ribbon, stitched by hand. Make a small bow from another piece of grosgrain ribbon and fringe the ends. Glue or stitch to the brim.

LOWER

Bright new headband.

Make a headband from a deep piece of braid (see page 10). I have used the reverse as I preferred the colors. Cover the back join with a piece of matching grosgrain ribbon.

◢ SECRETS

TRADE

If the straw has a tendency to stretch when you are straightening it out, run a line of machine stitching just below the edge before fitting the grosgrain ribbon.

Accentuate a Stylish Green Riding Hat

by covering with swirling silk, or encircling with tassel-wrapped paisley and bejewelled rayon

This elegant hat with its large brim needs bold trimmings to bring it to life.

You will need a half yard/half meter of dark green silk dupion. Remove the existing trimmings, then measure the outer edge of the brim, add seam allowances and cut a piece from the silk on the straight grain to this measurement and 10 in/25 cm deep.

Stitch the two short edges together. Attach the fabric, right side out, to the underside of the brim, stitching it about ¹/₂ in/1.5 cm away from the edge.

Fold the fabric over onto the top of the brim. Pull it at an angle to swirl round the brim. Gather into folds and tack round the headfitting line.

Cut another strip of silk 12 in/30 cm deep. Pin it at the base of the crown and draw round the hat, twisting and bunching it as you go. Turn under both long edges. Stitch in place to cover the raw edges of the previous strip.

Cut a third strip from the remaining width. Gather one short end, then roll up the strip into a flat spiral, hiding the two raw edges as you do so. Stitch to hold. Stitch the rose in place to cover the join in the headband.

variations on a theme

TOP
Added sparkle.

You will need 1 yard/1 meter of rayon novelty glitter fabric. Cut bias strips across the width, approximately 6 in/15 cm wide. Cut one strip in half lengthways, then fold all the strips in half. Place the half strip with one short end at the center back of the crown near the top. Stitch in place, then bring round to the bottom front of the crown and stitch down. Trim the excess. Place a full strip so that it covers the first one at the back, then bring the ends to the bottom front, overlapping them in a 'V' shape. Trim the excess. Repeat with the second full strip, placing it slightly lower than the previous one. Turn under the raw edges of the bottom strip. Make a bow from one of the remaining strips, cut to 14 in/35.5 cm (see page 50). Run a gathering thread through the middle and draw up. To make the tails, make another tube, 9 in/23 cm long. Turn in the raw edges at the short ends and hand stitch in place.

Place the bow over the tails and secure in the center. Embroider four or five rhinestones to each of the bow loops and tails. Embroider green crystal beads round the edges, then green and white crystal beads scattered over the rest of the space. Make a knot to bind the center of the bow (see page 57) and attach to the hat.

LOWER
Tassel-wrapped paisley.

Measure the crown of the hat and add 1 in/2.5 cm. Cut a piece of wool paisley to this measurement and 10 in/25 cm wide. Stitch the back join and fold under 1 in/2.5 cm on both long edges. At one side of the band, run a vertical gathering thread through the depth and pull up loosely. Place the band over the crown. Place a small tieback tassel over the gathered section of the headband and loop the ends over the band, one over and under and one in the opposite direction. Stitch the ends of the loops to the band at the back.

A Black Trilby Transformed

by adding easily made, sculptured feathers and a fabric flower in a mellow brown with a matching headband

The black trilby which is rather plain and ordinary before any embellishments.

Remove any trimmings, then cut the crown away from the brim $^3/_8$ in/1 cm above the head ribbon stitching line, leaving enough felt on the lower piece to stitch onto at a later stage. Measure the circumference of the edge of the brim and cut a strip of black moiré to this length plus seam allowances and $3^1/_2$ in/9 cm wide. Fold the strip in half, wrong sides together, then place against the brim with the raw edges against the brim, starting and finishing at center back. Fold the seam allowances under neatly. Tack, then stitch $^3/_8$ in/1 cm away from the edge all round. Fold over the brim to the underside and slip stitch by hand along the previous stitching line. Finish the back join by hand.

For the crown, measure the circumference of the head fitting line. Cut a strip from millinery buckram to this length plus seam allowance and $3^1/_2$ in/9 cm deep. Overlap the back seam and back stitch, making a circle. Bind the top and bottom edges with a bias strip of woven interfacing $1^1/_4$ in/3 cm wide (see page 72). Cover the whole buckram circle with a bias strip of interfacing, butting the back join to save bulkiness. Turn the raw edges to the wrong side and glue into place. Repeat to cover the padded circle with moiré taffeta but instead of butting the back join, make a neat seam.

Place the cut-off crown inside this moiré covered band, so that there is about 1 in/2.5 cm overlap. It should fit tightly. Tack, then glue in place and leave to set. Hold the crown over a steaming kettle (keeping your hands clear of the steam) and pinch the ridge at the top of the hat to emphasize it.

Finally, fit the brim inside the new band and slip stitch in place, concealing the stitches behind the original head ribbon. Fit the rose and headband as described opposite.

making a gathered rose and headband

❶ Measure the head fitting and cut a piece of 1 in/2.5 cm wide grosgrain ribbon to this length plus a little overlap. Cut a piece of top fabric 2¹/₄ in/6 cm wide and to the same length. Place the ribbon in the center of the wrong side of the fabric strip. Tack in place, then fold the raw edges over to the back and glue in place.

❷ Cut a strip of top fabric 4 in/10 cm wide across the width of the chosen fabric (e.g. 36 in/90 cm long). Fold in half lengthwise with wrong sides together. Trim and stitch both ends so that they taper.

❸ Gather along the raw edge a short way, then pull up and begin to wrap into a rose shape. The ribbon can be loosely or tightly wrapped over to make the size of the rose required.

❹ Stitch at the base to hold and continue in this way until the whole strip has been gathered and curled.

❺ Place the covered grosgrain ribbon round the hat, overlap the two raw edges at the front and stitch, then stitch on the rose to hide the join in the ribbon. Keep the stitches as small as possible.

using the basic makeover a variety of stunning options can

1

1 Fun with feathers.
Fit three groups of small white feathers and one large one behind the rosette. Secure with a small safety pin.

2 Stripes and spots.
Measure the circumference of the crown and cut a piece of 1 in/2.5 cm wide spotted ribbon to this measurement plus seam allowances. Stitch the back seam to make into a headband.

Cut a piece of striped cotton 5 1/2 x 14 in/ 14 x 36 cm. Fold the long edges in to the center and press. Cut a second piece of spotted ribbon 14 in/ 36 cm long. Spray with glue and place centrally over the striped cotton to hold in place. Bring the two short edges to the center at the back. Pinch in at the center and cut a narrow strip of striped fabric about 2 1/4 in/6 cm wide, fold in the ends and fold round the center of the bow.

Attach the bow to the spotted headband, concealing the stitches at the back and place over the hat.

3 Knitted yarn garland.
Use peacock jade chenille yarn. Take a ruler and knot the yarn round one end, then cast on along the length of the ruler, as though knitting. Make a length that will go twice round the hat.

Tie off, take the loops

```
2 | 3
-----
4 | 5
```

off the ruler, double up and stitch together at the base, then pull round the hat and stitch down at the back. Stitch antique buttons evenly spaced round the headband.

4 Flower power.
Cut a strip, 1¹/₂ x 20 in/ 4 x 50 cm from millinery buckram. Cut a strip 4 x 20 in/10 x 50 cm from black moiré taffeta. Use to cover the buckram (see page 66). Form into a double loop. Stitch flowers over the loop at the base, then attach to the hat at the side.

5 Rouleau cockade.
Cut ten bias strips of white satin, 9 x 1¹/₄ in/ 23 x 3 cm. Stitch into narrow rouleaux (see page 74). Group together in loops to form a cockade. Cut a piece of satin 2¹/₂ x 1¹/₄ in/6 x 3 cm. Turn in one short edge, then turn over the two long edges. Attach the raw edge to the base of the rouleaux, wind it round and slip stitch the folded edge down. Stitch to the front of the hat.

For the headband, cut a bias piece of white satin the circumference of the crown plus seam allowances and 2 in/5 cm deep. Bond a strip of 1 in/2.5 cm wide gros-grain ribbon centrally to the satin (see page 74). Turn in all the edges to the wrong side. Fit round the hat, short edges butting, and whip stitch.

Be Extravagant with an Exotic Straw Hat

by adding lavish organdie leaves, wonderful ostrich feathers and glittering metallic tulle

Such a good color and shape as this needs trimmings to match.

Fold 1 yard/1 meter of white cotton organdie into four across the width, then, using the templates provided (page 78), cut out as many leaf shapes in the three sizes as you can. Roll both long edges of each shape onto the right side of the fabric as described on page 56. Put a little pleat in the short edge to narrow it and finger-press to hold.

Pin a circle of the largest leaves round the hat towards the top of the crown, so that they hang just below the crown and stab stitch in place. Stitch another circle of medium-sized leaves above this one, so that they hang just short of the first layer. Continue in this way until the crown is richly filled, using the smallest leaves at the top. Cover the raw edges at the top with a dome-shaped button covered in white satin and organdie.

Spray with a fine mist of fabric stiffener to hold the leaves in shape.

For a more elaborate effect, you could paint the rolled edges with fabric paint, so that they look as if they have been piped in a different color.

variations on a theme

TOP
Wreathed in tulle.
*From a yard/meter of metallic tulle, cut five
7 in/18 cm strips across the width. Fold each
in half lengthways. Using double thread,
gather along the folded edge, joining the
strips together by overlapping them. Pull up
loosely.*

*To attach to the hat, pin one end at the
lower (folded) edge to the base of the crown,
then take up to the top of the crown and pin.
Take down again and pin, then repeat this
zigzag arrangement all round the crown.
Adjust the pins so that the zigzags are even
and when you are satisfied with the arrangement, stab stitch in place. Pull open the two
raw edges of the ruffle and fluff out.*

LOWER
Circled with feathers.
*Take an ostrich feather boa and pin one end
to the tip of the crown, pinning from the
inside. Wind the boa round the hat in a
spiral. On the last round, fold the boa back
on itself to expose some of the hat. Stitch in
place from the inside.*

Tricks of the Trade

Removing head ribbon

The head ribbon is made up to your headfitting size. It's made from grosgrain ribbon $1/2$ - 1 in/1.5 - 2.5 cm wide and is stitched inside the hat at the base of the crown (where the hat sits on the head, called the head fitting line). To remove, simply unpick the stitches and iron to freshen.

Replacing head ribbon

Cotton or cotton mix grosgrain ribbon is best because it shapes more easily and is stiffer. Buy $3/4$ yard/$3/4$ meter. If the old ribbon was a good fit, cut a new one to the same size. If not, take your head measure-

ment round your forehead plus seam allowances. Curve it to shape the crown of the hat (see below) and slip stitch to the hat with long stitches along the bottom edge. Turn in both raw edges at the back, butt up the two ends and whip stitch about half way up the join.

Curving ribbon

Lay the piece of ribbon flat on an ironing board. Hold one end in one hand and pull it gently to curve as you iron with the other hand.

Adding an easing thread to a head ribbon

Use garter elastic and stitch it behind the top of the free edge of the grosgrain ribbon stretching it slightly to fit your headfitting size.

Steaming and brushing felt

Brush with a good, stiff clothes brush to get rid of dust and flecks, then hold it carefully over the steam from a kettle for a few seconds. Be very careful not to burn your fingers. Leave to dry, then brush again.

Altering the shape by steaming

If you want to make a con-vexed crease across the tip of the crown, hold the hat care-fully over the steam from a kettle and make the crease with your fingers but be very careful not to burn them. The process takes just a few seconds. Leave

to dry. You can do the same if you want an upswept brim. Mist with fabric spray to hold.

Binding with woven interfacing

Buy a yard/meter of woven interfacing. Fold the top left hand corner down to the sel-vage to find the bias, then cut across parallel to the fold about 8 in/20 cm away from it. Fold the strip in half and half again, repeating until the piece is roughly 8 in/20 cm square. Pin to secure, then draw lines about

$3/4$ in/2 cm wide parallel to the cut edge. Cut off a strip. Pull the strip lengthways to take out the stretch. Fold in half length-ways, place over the edge to be bound, then attach with a long running stitch.

Reviving straw

Brush with a soft brush to remove any particles of dust trapped in the straw, then freshen in steam as for felt. Allow to dry, then coat with cellulose dope (varnish), as used by model makers and sold in craft shops. If the wire is out of shape, remove, cut a new wire and replace (see below).

Removing wire from straw

The wire may be zigzag-stitched on to the straw in a

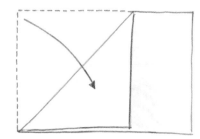

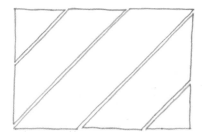

PARTS OF A HAT

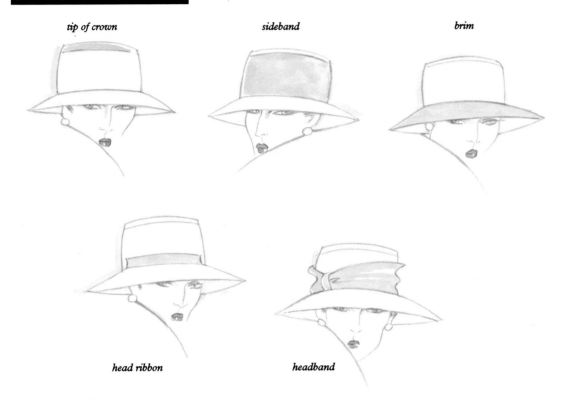

tip of crown   *sideband*   *brim*

head ribbon   *headband*

buckram on the underside close to the stitching. If covering with a fine fabric, stitch a bias strip of woven interfacing (see above) over the seam to even out the join. Cover the base with woven interfacing.

Cut a circle of soft interfacing. Depending on the height of the cone, you should be able to pull it smoothly over the surface without a seam. Turn the raw edges to the under side and glue in place. Cover in the same way with a circle of the chosen top fabric.

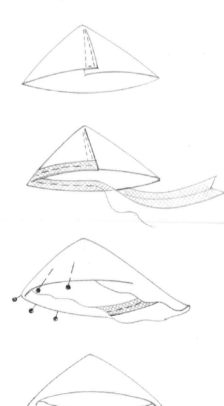

casing of muslin or ribbon or simply zigzag-stitched in place. Unpick the stitching and remove the wire.

Millinery wire is wound on a spool for sale, so you need to take out the bounce before using. Simply bend it away from the curve with your thumb and forefinger until it is straight. Wire stitch it to the inside edge of the brim, then cover with a curved piece of grosgrain ribbon. Overlap the ends of the ribbon and slip stitch in place.

Binding with sticky-backed ribbon

This ribbon is manufactured with a central wire down the length and strips of paper on either side, covering a sticky back. It is only suitable for binding straight edges. Cut to the size needed, then peel off one of the paper strips. Place the right side of the fabric to the sticky side, aligning the fabric edge with the wire. Press down, peel off the other strip of paper and fold the ribbon over the edge of the fabric to the

back and press in place.

When taking the ribbon round a sharp corner or right angle, snip a 'V' shape out of the ribbon on both sides, so that it will lie flat.

Making a cone

Cut out a circle from millinery buckram. Make a cut through to the center, then overlap the two edges to bring up the circle into a cone. The more you overlap, the steeper the sides of the cone will be. Back stitch the join, then trim off the excess

73

Tricks of the Trade

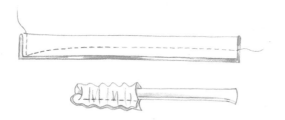

Making a rouleau

Cut bias strips of fabric (as above) to double the width of the finished rouleau plus seam allowances and to the required length. A narrow rouleau is cut about 1¼ in/ 3 cm wide.

Fold the strip in half lengthways, right sides together. Machine down the length, stitching the width of the machine foot away from the raw edges. At the end of the strip, take the stitching into the seam allowance then across the short end. (This makes it easier to turn through.) Trim the seam allowance. Turn through using a knitting needle or the point of a blunt pencil.

Cutting and joining a bias strip

Find the bias (as for woven interfacing) and cut a strip to the required width. Cut the edges on the straight grain, so

that they do not stretch. Join the seam with right sides together, trim and press open.

Stitching a French seam

To make a French seam, place the fabric wrong sides together, then stitch two-thirds the depth of the seam allowance. Trim off the excess close to the stitching. Turn the fabric so that right sides are together and stitch again along the seam line.

Using fusible web

Fusible web is good for bonding two fabrics together, which can then be cut without fraying. Follow the manufacturer's instructions and use the paper removed from the web to protect the fabric when ironing.

Adding a comb inside a small hat

Break a small curved comb in half. Take a piece of grosgrain ribbon twice the depth of the top edge of the comb plus seam allowances. Place centrally over the edge of the comb and fold in the seam allowances at both ends. Fold over the top edge of the ribbon, so that the top of the comb is covered with ribbon. Stitch the two short sides of the ribbon together, then stitch the two long edges together through the teeth of the comb and back up the remaining short side. Catch stitch the comb at the corners to the inside of the crown in the position required with the teeth facing the center of the crown.

HAT SHAPES

picture hat

bowler

boater

cloche

pill box

toque

breton

trilby

beret

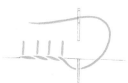

blanket stitch
for edge decoration

running stitch
for attaching one fabric
to another loosely

wire stitch
for attaching millinery
wire: a variation of blanket
stitch as shown above

stab stitch
for attaching one
fabric to another as
invisibly as possible

whip stitch
for joining together
thick fabrics, such as
fake fur or felt

back stitch
for attaching one fabric
to another securely

MATERIALS

Glue
Use a PVC glue suitable for fabrics but test on a spare piece first. Glueing two fabrics together is often a suitable and quick alternative to stitching.

Grosgrain ribbon
A corded ribbon used for headribbons and binding rounded shapes as it can easily be curved (see page 72). Use cotton or cotton mix, as this is easier to shape.

Interfacing
Use a soft, woollen variety, for padding over hard surfaces.

Millinery buckram
A stiff, coarse, openweave fabric, available in black and white, used to make foundation shapes.

Millinery wire
Used for stiffening edges or making trimmings, this wire is covered in thread and sold in various thicknesses. Fine is the most commonly available and is the gauge I have used .

Peachbloom felt
A good quality felt with a soft pile which is usually brushed in one direction.

Sinamay
A fine, stiff, openweave fabric woven from the fibres of the banana plant. It can be dampened, then molded to shape. Once it dries, it holds its new shape but should not be allowed to get wet again in rain.

Straw
There are many different types of straw used for hat-

making. The list below describes the straw hats appearing in this book.

- exotic: woven from high quality straw, such as Manila, Panama or parabuntal. The finish is smooth and glossy.
- imitation: woven from cellophane thread.
- Italian: made from straw woven into braids which are then stitched together to produce the hat body which is then blocked into shape. The brims are flexible and can be worn up or down.
- paper: made from paper pulp formed into thread which can then be woven.

Woven interfacing
A fine stretchy net used for binding edges, as it shapes easily round curves.

tacking stitch
for holding two pieces of fabric
together temporarily

herringbone stitch
for loosely holding a seam
allowance in place

grafting stitch
for attaching two pieces
of lace together

slip stitch
for hemming

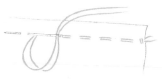

gathering stitch
for pulling up a fabric into
gathers: use a double thread

holding stitch
for anchoring ruched
fabric in position

Templates

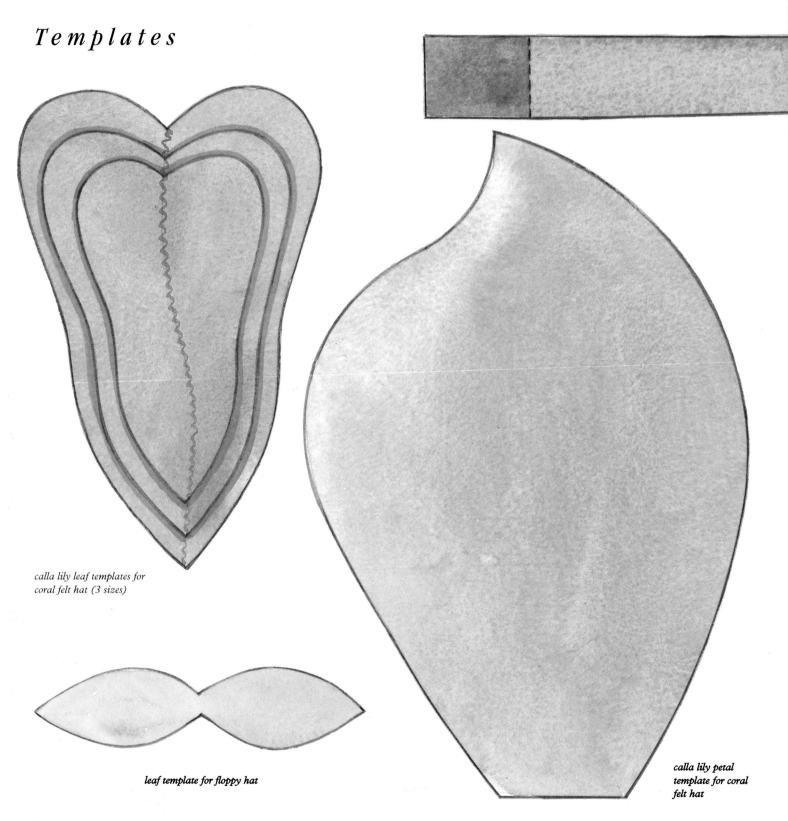

calla lily leaf templates for
coral felt hat (3 sizes)

leaf template for floppy hat

**calla lily petal
template for coral
felt hat**

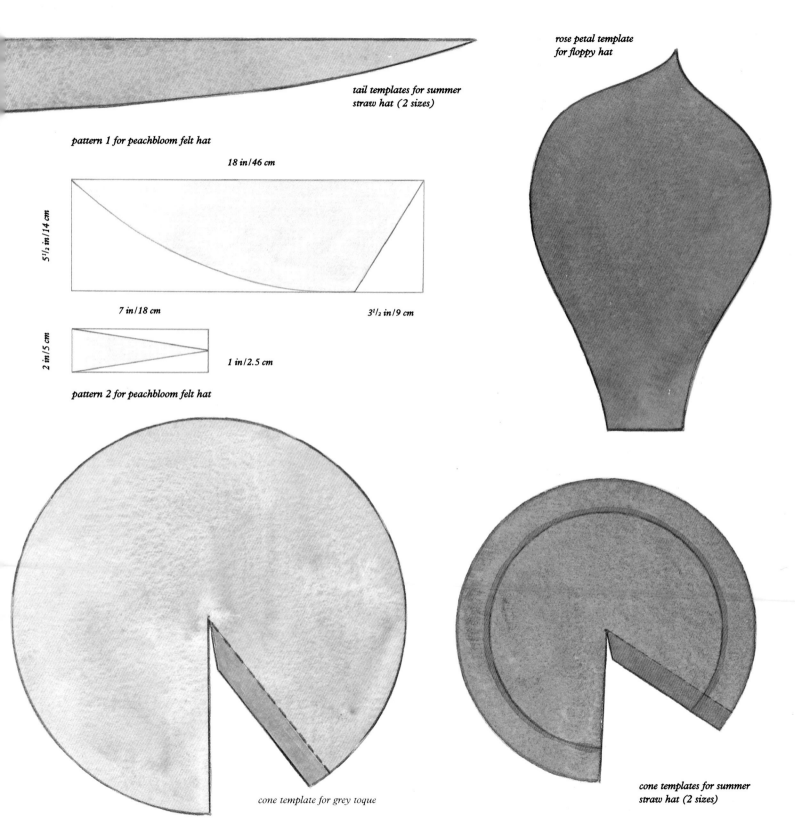

tail templates for summer
straw hat (2 sizes)

pattern 1 for peachbloom felt hat

18 in/46 cm

5¹/₂ in/14 cm

7 in/18 cm

3¹/₂ in/9 cm

2 in/5 cm

1 in/2.5 cm

pattern 2 for peachbloom felt hat

rose petal template
for floppy hat

cone template for grey toque

cone templates for summer
straw hat (2 sizes)

Templates

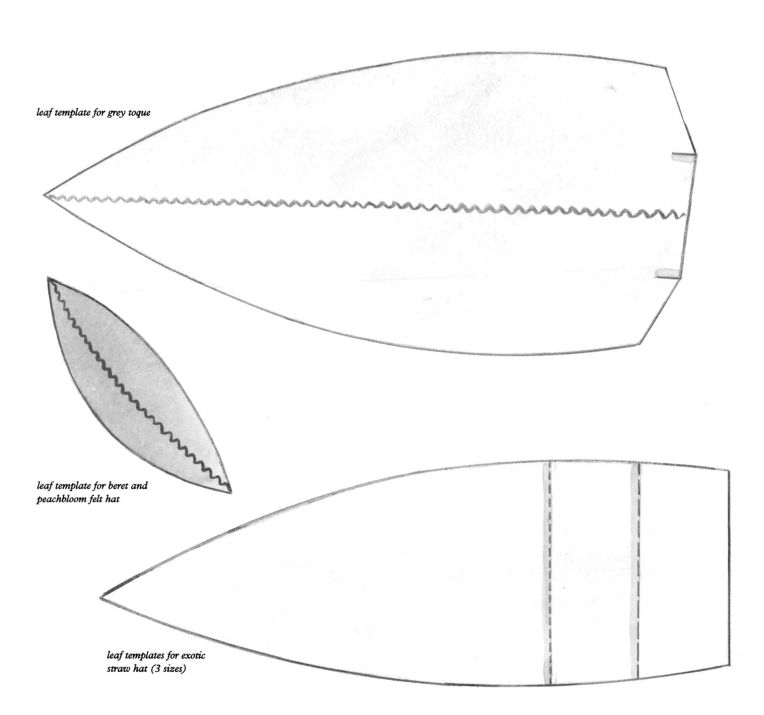

leaf template for grey toque

leaf template for beret and
peachbloom felt hat

leaf templates for exotic
straw hat (3 sizes)

Index

ACKNOWLEDGEMENTS
*With many thanks to the
following for donating hats
from the back of their
wardrobes:
Meg Abdy; Elizabeth Forster;
Yvonne McFarlane; Rosemary
Wilkinson and Susan Williams.
Thanks also to Katie Gayle for
supplying the papier mâché
pins and brooches for the hat
on page 39; to Rosie Tucker
for the knitting yarns used
throughout; to Shona for
taking excellent photographs;
to Rosemary for translating
my making-up notes and
to Mike for creating the book
design.*